AF228792

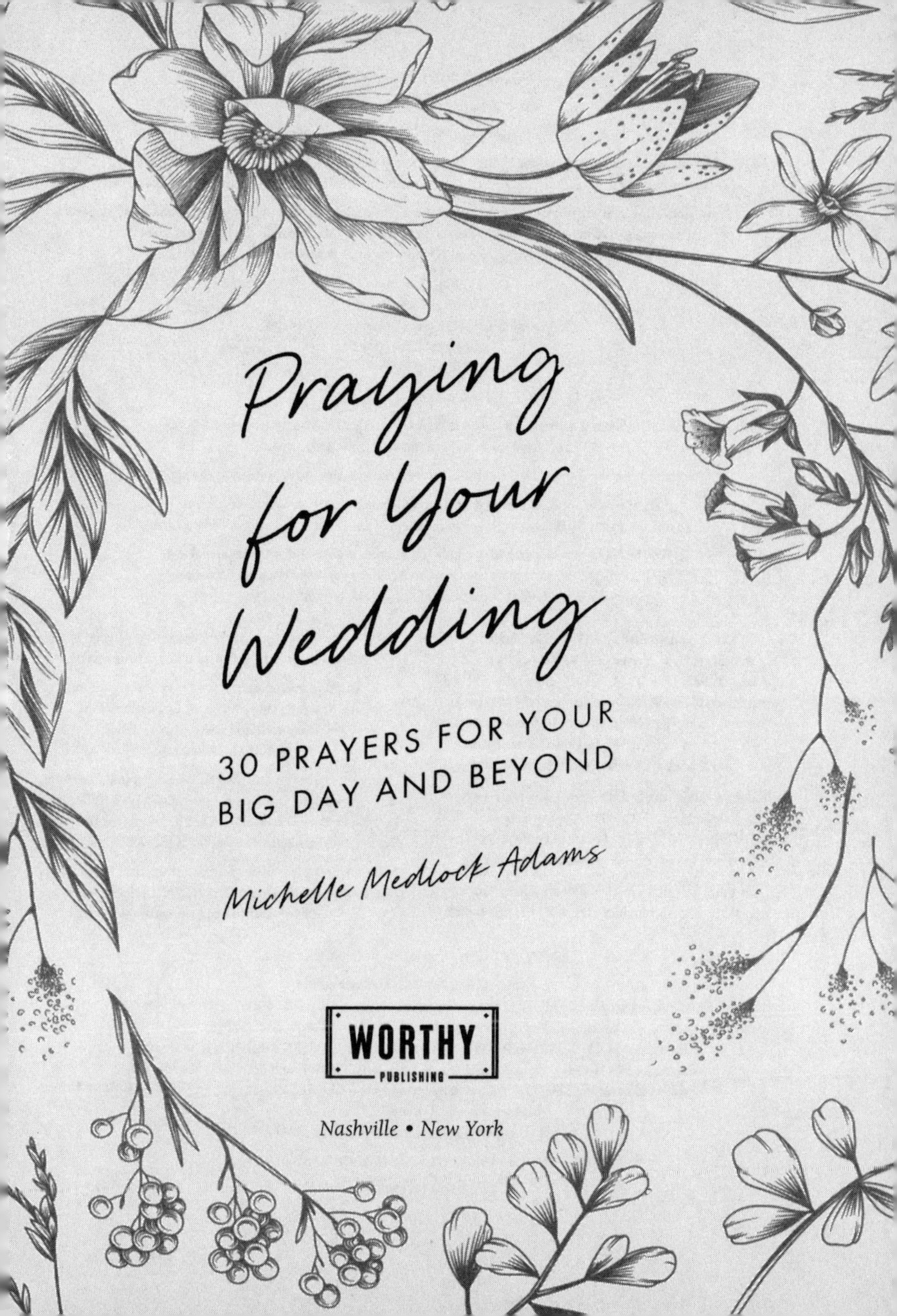

Praying for Your Wedding

30 PRAYERS FOR YOUR BIG DAY AND BEYOND

Michelle Medlock Adams

WORTHY
PUBLISHING

Nashville • New York

Worthy Books
Hachette Book Group
1290 Avenue of the Americas, New York, NY 10104
worthypublishing.com
@WorthyPub

First Edition: May 2026

Worthy Books is a division of Hachette Book Group, Inc. The Worthy name and logo are registered trademarks of Hachette Book Group, Inc.

The publisher is not responsible for websites (or their content) that are not owned by the publisher.

The Hachette Speakers Bureau provides a wide range of authors for speaking events. To find out more, visit hachettespeakersbureau.com or email HachetteSpeakers@hbgusa.com.

Worthy Books may be purchased in bulk for business, educational, or promotional use. For information, please contact your local bookseller or email the Hachette Book Group Special Markets Department at Special.Markets@hbgusa.com.

Library of Congress Cataloging-in-Publication Data

Name: Adams, Michelle Medlock author
Title: Praying for your wedding: 30 prayers for your big day and beyond / Michelle Medlock Adams.
Description: First edition. | Nashville; New York: Worthy Books, 2026.
Identifiers: LCCN 2025047409 | ISBN 9781546011507 board | ISBN 9781546011668 ebook
Subjects: LCSH: Anxiety—Religious aspects—Christianity—Prayers and devotions | Weddings—Prayers and devotions | Mate selection—Religious aspects—Christianity—Prayers and devotions
Classification: LCC BV4908.5 .A336 2026
LC record available at https://lccn.loc.gov/2025047409

ISBNs: 978-1-546-01150-7 (paper over board); 978-1-546-01166-8 (ebook)

Printed in Canada

MRQ

10 9 8 7 6 5 4 3 2 1

CONTENTS

Contents

HOW TO USE THIS BOOK

Congratulations! Whether you're recently engaged, in full-on wedding planning mode, or newly married, this is such an exciting season, isn't it? But it can be a stressful one, too. Philippians 4:6 says, "Do not be anxious about anything, but in every situation, by prayer and petition, with thanksgiving, present your requests to God" (NIV). So that's what we're doing for the next thirty days.

Use this book as a prayer guide as you navigate these new waters. As you'll see, each prayer entry is specific to your wedding planning, your actual wedding day, your husband, or your new marriage. Each day's entry also includes several scriptures that relate to that day's prayer. Why did I include these? Because if we pray according to God's Word, then we pray correctly and powerfully. It's good to read these verses and even commit them to memory. I encourage you to write out your own prayers based on the daily scriptures on the lines provided and jot down specific prayer requests and praises surrounding that day's theme.

Each day's prayer also includes a "Say It" section. This is simply a bold statement you can declare to cement what you've just prayed. "Faith comes by hearing and hearing by the Word of God," so to hear yourself praying aloud, reading the related scriptures, and saying that bold statement, you are building your faith in that area. Isn't that good news?

Lastly, when you pray, pray believing. Pray expecting! Thank God for the desired result as if it's already happened and then trust Him with your requests because He has your best interest at heart.

I'm so happy for you! Enjoy this special season and use this prayer book to grow closer to God throughout the planning, marrying, and embarking on your new life with your soulmate.

Prayer That I Have No Anxiety Leading Up to Our Wedding

"Cast all your anxiety on Him because He cares for you."

(1 Peter 5:7, NIV)

PRAY IT

$\mathcal{F}$ather God, Your Word says to cast all my cares onto You, and I ask for Your help as I prepare for our wedding. There are just so many details to juggle, LORD, and it is easy to worry so much about the small things. Help me to prioritize tasks, delegate duties, and stand firm on my desires. Help me to make decisions with ease and not to flip-flop on my choices once they are made. And help me, God, to see things clearly, to breathe deeply, and to face urgent decisions with a calmness that comes only from You. Please give me discernment so that I can be confident in the plans we are making and maintain peace throughout the entire process. More than anything, LORD, help me to remember that we are preparing for a marriage, not just a wedding. Please help me to lean into You and rest in Your supernatural peace so that I can enjoy this journey. I love You, LORD, amen.

SAY IT

I do not allow the stresses and worries of wedding planning to steal my joy; instead, I rest in God's supernatural peace today.

MEDITATE ON IT

"Now may the LORD of peace Himself give you peace at all times in every way. The LORD be with you all."
(2 Thessalonians 3:16, ESV)

"And let the peace of Christ rule in your hearts, to which indeed you were called in one body. And be thankful."
(Colossians 3:15, ESV)

"And the peace of God, which surpasses all understanding, will guard your hearts and your minds in Christ Jesus."
(Philippians 4:7, ESV)

Prayer for Unity

"How good and pleasant it is when
God's people live together in unity!"

(Psalm 133:1, NIV)

PRAY IT

$\mathcal{F}$ather God, I pray that You unite my heart to my husband's heart with Your great love—not only on our wedding day but also through our entire lives. I realize we might not see eye to eye on every issue, but, LORD, help us to believe the best about each other and treat each other with respect—even when we disagree. And, LORD, I also pray that You join our two families in a beautiful forever kind of way. Help us to see our differences as strengths and help us to find common ground as we begin this process of becoming one family. Thank You, God, for expanding my circle of love. I am truly blessed. I love You, LORD, amen.

SAY IT

*I choose love not just on our wedding day but
throughout our marriage, and I trust God to
bring our families together so we can enjoy
a lifetime of unity, love, and joy.*

MEDITATE ON IT

"If a house is divided against itself, that house cannot stand."
(Mark 3:25, NIV)

"Above all, love each other deeply, because love covers over a
multitude of sins. Offer hospitality to one another without
grumbling." (1 Peter 4:8–9, NIV)

"I want them to be encouraged and knit together by strong
ties of love. I want them to have complete confidence that
they understand God's mysterious plan, which is Christ
Himself." (Colossians 2:2, NLT)

Prayer for Lasting Love

"Trust in the LORD with all your
heart, and do not lean on your own
understanding. In all your ways
acknowledge Him, and He will make
straight your paths."

(PROVERBS 3:5–6, ESV)

PRAY IT

Heavenly Father, help me to remember that we are not planning just for one day but rather for a lifetime together. We commit all our plans to You, LORD. Your Word says that You will direct our steps, and we praise You for that promise. Thank You, God, for leading me to this incredible person I get to marry. Open the eyes of my heart so I can see my husband the way that You see him—today, on our wedding day, during our honeymoon, and always. LORD, I pray that I never forget the reasons I fell in love with my husband and that he never forgets the reasons he chose me. Help us to grow more in love every day, as we keep You at the center of our marriage. I ask all this in the Mighty Name of Jesus. Amen.

SAY IT

*I commit my plans, my hopes, and my dreams to God.
And I vow to love my husband with my whole
heart all the days of my life.*

MEDITATE ON IT

"We can make our plans, but the LORD determines our steps."
(Proverbs 16:9, NLT)

"The LORD directs the steps of the godly. He delights in every
detail of their lives." (Psalm 37:23, NLT)

"Dear friends, let us continue to love one another, for love
comes from God. Anyone who loves is a child of God and
knows God." (1 John 4:7, NLT)

Prayer of Thanks for Leading Me to My Future Husband

"Now, our God, we give You thanks,
and praise Your glorious name."

(1 Chronicles 29:13, NIV)

PRAY IT

$\mathcal{F}$ather God, thank You for leading me to my soulmate, my forever love, my best friend, and the person in life who truly gets me. How can I ever praise You enough for all that You have done for me? I pray that my husband knows how very much You love him and that he realizes how very much I adore him. Help me to love him like You do, God. And help the two of us to fall deeper in love every single day. You have blessed me above and beyond, LORD, and I am so very grateful. You are such a good God. I love You. Amen.

SAY IT

I take time each day to thank God for giving me such an amazing person. And I make sure I tell my husband how much I appreciate him daily.

MEDITATE ON IT

"I always thank my God for you because of His grace given you in Christ Jesus." (1 Corinthians 1:4, NIV)

"Every good and perfect gift is from above, coming down from the Father of the heavenly lights, who does not change like shifting shadows." (James 1:17, NIV)

"Always giving thanks to God the Father for everything, in the name of our LORD Jesus Christ." (Ephesians 5:20, NIV)

Prayer for Special Moments on Our Wedding Day

"This is the day the LORD has made;
We will rejoice and be glad in it."

(PSALM 118:24, NKJV)

PRAY IT

$\mathcal{F}$ather God, thank You for allowing all the important people in my life to celebrate with me on our wedding day. I am so grateful, LORD. I praise You for putting such amazing people in my life. Please help me to navigate the day in such a way that I'll have meaningful moments with all the people who are coming to celebrate with me. Help me to really connect with each person and make lasting memories. And, LORD, help me to express to everyone how much they mean to me. I want to look back on these encounters with my loved ones and smile. Thank You, God, for this day and for surrounding me with such incredible people who love me. I love You. Amen.

SAY IT

*I will do my best on our wedding day to connect with
the people who mean the most to me. I will cherish each
moment and be grateful for their support and
love on such an important day.*

MEDITATE ON IT

"Teach us to number our days, that we may gain a heart of
wisdom." (Psalm 90:12, NIV)

"Let us think of ways to motivate one another to acts of
love and good works. And let us not neglect our meeting
together, as some people do, but encourage one another,
especially now that the day of His return is drawing near."
(Hebrews 10:24–25, NLT)

"This is my commandment: Love each other in the same way
I have loved you." (John 15:12, NLT)

Prayer That My Husband and I Grow in Faith Together

"All Scripture is God-breathed and is useful for teaching, rebuking, correcting and training in righteousness, so that the servant of God may be thoroughly equipped for every good work."

(2 Timothy 3:16–17, NIV)

PRAY IT

𝓕ather God, I pray that my husband and I fall in love with Your Word and partake of it daily. Help us both to crave Your Word the same way we crave food. Help us to think about it all day long, meditating on Your promises. I pray that we read it and make it the final authority in our life together. LORD, help the two of us to find time to read the Bible together and build our marriage on the firm foundation of Your promises. Help us to see spending time in Your Word as a privilege, not an obligation, as something that brings us closer together as a couple. Help us to grow in our faith together, both in the process of planning this wedding and in the months and years to come. Thank You, God, for Your Word. Amen.

SAY IT

*I pray for my husband to fall in love with God's Word and
that I find time to read and study God's Word every day.*

MEDITATE ON IT

"Your Word is a lamp for my feet, a light on my path."
   (Psalm 119:105, NIV)

"Heaven and earth will pass away, but My Words will never
   pass away." (Matthew 24:35, NIV)

"I have hidden Your Word in my heart that I might not sin
   against You." (Psalm 119:11, NIV)

Prayer That I Manage Expectations

"So humble yourselves under the mighty power of God, and at the right time He will lift you up in honor. Give all your worries and cares to God, for He cares about you."

(1 Peter 5:6–7, NLT)

Father God, I pray that I do not overthink everything regarding our upcoming wedding day. Help me, God, to keep my expectations manageable in my quest to create the wedding I've always dreamed of, and help me to remain grateful throughout the planning process. I give the pressure I'm feeling to pull off the perfect wedding to You, LORD. I am casting all my cares on You, as Your Word instructs, and I am asking You to fill my heart with supernatural peace. I am not planning for just one day but rather for a lifetime of love, so help me, LORD, to keep that in mind when all the wedding day details seem overwhelming. I commit to fixing my eyes on You today, tomorrow, and every day, especially in the days leading up to our wedding. I love You, God. Amen.

SAY IT

I will fix my eyes on God throughout the wedding planning process, and I will have a grateful heart no matter what.

MEDITATE ON IT

"Therefore I tell you, do not worry about your life, what you will eat or drink; or about your body, what you will wear. Is not life more than food, and the body more than clothes?" (Matthew 6:25, NIV)

"I am not saying this because I am in need, for I have learned to be content whatever the circumstances. I know what it is to be in need, and I know what it is to have plenty. I have learned the secret of being content in any and every situation, whether well fed or hungry, whether living in plenty or in want. I can do all this through Him who gives me strength." (Philippians 4:11–13, NIV)

"Trust in the LORD and do good; dwell in the land and enjoy safe pasture. Take delight in the LORD, and He will give you the desires of your heart." (Psalm 37:3–4, NIV)

"But seek first His kingdom and His righteousness, and all these things will be given to you as well." (Matthew 6:33, NIV)

Prayer That I Have Patience

*"Rejoice always, pray continually, give
thanks in all circumstances; for this is
God's will for you in Christ Jesus."*

(1 Thessalonians 5:16–18, NIV)

Father God, I pray that I keep everything in perspective and see things through Your eyes as I prepare for the big day. Help me to be gracious and kind through my words and actions when dealing with family, friends, my future husband, the wedding party, and the vendors. And, LORD, build in me a grateful heart. Help me to find reasons to be thankful every single day leading up to the wedding, and after as well. Father, when situations become stressful or things don't work out as planned, help me to be reasonable and agreeable. Help me to resist the urge to be a "bridezilla" and instead let Your love shine through me. I ask these things in the Name of Your Son, Jesus. Amen.

SAY IT

*I choose to be kind, gentle, and agreeable no matter what
happens. I choose to be grateful in all things.*

MEDITATE ON IT

"Therefore, as God's chosen people, holy and dearly loved,
clothe yourselves with compassion, kindness, humility,
gentleness and patience." (Colossians 3:12, NIV)

"Gracious words are a honeycomb, sweet to the soul and
healing to the bones." (Proverbs 16:24, NIV)

"Finally, all of you, be like-minded, be sympathetic, love one
another, be compassionate and humble." (1 Peter 3:8, NIV)

"But seek first His kingdom and His righteousness, and
all these things will be given to you as well."
(Matthew 6:33, NIV)

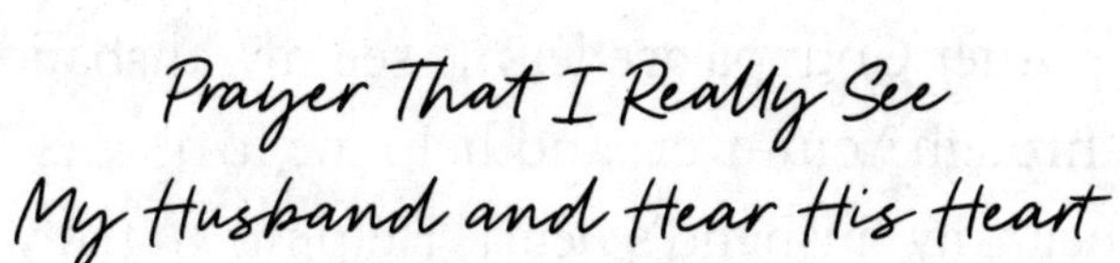

Prayer That I Really See My Husband and Hear His Heart

"I pray that the eyes of your heart may be enlightened in order that you may know the hope to which He has called you, the riches of His glorious inheritance in His holy people, and His incomparably great power for us who believe. That power is the same as the mighty strength."

(EPHESIANS 1:18–19, NIV)

PRAY IT

$\mathcal{F}$ather God, please let me see my husband through Your eyes, and help me to always hear my husband's heart. Help me to truly listen to him when he shares his hopes and dreams—not just wait for my chance to talk—but help me to truly focus on what he is saying. And, LORD, give me a gentle and supportive spirit toward him. I pray that we grow together, put You first, and build a beautiful life, side by side. I'm excited about this upcoming chapter, and I'm so grateful that You have given me such an amazing man to be my husband. Thank You, God. Amen.

SAY IT

*I choose to see the best in my husband, and I vow to
love him and support him today, tomorrow,
and for the rest of our lives.*

MEDITATE ON IT

"The LORD God said, 'It is not good for the man to be alone. I
will make a helper suitable for him.'" (Genesis 2:18, NIV)

"Two are better than one, because they have a good return for
their labor: If either of them falls down, one can help the
other up. But pity anyone who falls and has no one to help
them up. Also, if two lie down together, they will keep
warm. But how can one keep warm alone?"
(Ecclesiastes 4:9–11, NIV)

"As a prisoner for the LORD, then, I urge you to live a life
worthy of the calling you have received. Be completely
humble and gentle; be patient, bearing with one another
in love. Make every effort to keep the unity of the Spirit
through the bond of peace." (Ephesians 4:1–3, NIV)

"May the God who gives endurance and encouragement give
you the same attitude of mind toward each other that
Christ Jesus had." (Romans 15:5, NIV)

Prayer That My Husband Truly Knows Who He Is in Christ Jesus

"Therefore, if anyone is in Christ, the new creation has come: The old has gone, the new is here!"

(2 Corinthians 5:17, NIV)

PRAY IT

*F*ather God, I pray that my husband falls in love with You and Your Word and that he comes to know You in a deeper, more meaningful way. Your Word says that Your sheep know Your voice, so I pray that my husband hears Your voice clearly, above all other voices, and that he follows Your leading in all things. Help him, LORD, to truly know who he is in You. Help him to realize his worth. And help him to understand that, through You and with You, he can accomplish big things and walk in his calling with an energetic confidence. Thank You, God, for loving him and loving me with an unconditional, everlasting love. Amen.

SAY IT

*I commit to pray for my husband daily and
encourage him in his walk with Christ.*

MEDITATE ON IT

"Don't you know that you yourselves are God's temple and
that God's Spirit dwells in your midst?"
(1 Corinthians 3:16, NIV)

"You yourselves are our letter, written on our hearts, known and
read by everyone. You show that you are a letter from Christ,
the result of our ministry, written not with ink but with
the Spirit of the living God, not on tablets of stone but on
tablets of human hearts. Such confidence we have through
Christ before God." (2 Corinthians 3:2–4, NIV)

"For God, who said, 'Let light shine out of darkness,' made
His light shine in our hearts to give us the light of the
knowledge of God's glory displayed in the face of Christ."
(2 Corinthians 4:6, NIV)

Prayer for a Seamless Flow on Our Wedding Day

"But seek first His kingdom and His righteousness, and all these things will be provided to you."

(Matthew 6:33, NASB)

PRAY IT

$\mathcal{F}$ather God, I give You every single detail of our upcoming wedding day—help me not to stress over any part of it. I pray that there is a seamless flow on our big day from beginning to end. I pray that we have great weather; I pray that everyone is happy and healthy; and I pray that everything turns out beautifully. LORD, the plans we're making and the money we're spending to bring this day into fruition, I ask that You bless all of it. Help it all to come together, and even if something unexpected happens, I pray that we just roll with it and embrace the unexpected. Lastly, I ask that You be in every aspect of the day. Help me to feel Your presence. I love You, amen.

SAY IT

*I will do everything in my power to make our
wedding day run smoothly, but even if it doesn't, I
choose to embrace the unexpected and rejoice
in the extraordinary day.*

MEDITATE ON IT

"Then Jesus said to His disciples: 'Therefore I tell you, do not worry about your life, what you will eat; or about your body, what you will wear. For life is more than food, and the body more than clothes. Consider the ravens: They do not sow or reap, they have no storeroom or barn; yet God feeds them. And how much more valuable you are than birds! Who of you by worrying can add a single hour to your life?'" (Luke 12:22–25, NIV)

"In their hearts humans plan their course, but the LORD establishes their steps." (Proverbs 16:9, NIV)

"May the God of hope fill you with all joy and peace as you trust in Him, so that you may overflow with hope by the power of the Holy Spirit." (Romans 15:13, NIV)

Prayer That I Do Not Fall into the Comparison Trap

"Since we live by the Spirit, let us keep in step with the Spirit. Let us not become conceited, provoking and envying each other."

(GALATIANS 5:25–26, NIV)

$\mathcal{F}$ather God, I'm finding it difficult not to compare myself with other brides, and I'm having trouble not comparing our upcoming wedding to the Pinterest-perfect versions I see online. Help me, LORD, to avoid falling into that comparison trap, measuring my worth and beauty against others'. Help me to be content with myself and confident in my appearance. And, Father, I'm asking that You keep my eyes focused on You. Help me to stop scrolling through other couples' wedding décor and ceremonies, comparing their venue, flowers, table décor, and wedding party with what we're planning. Rather, LORD, help me to be grateful for the many blessings in my life and content in all things, especially the choices we make regarding our upcoming wedding. I love You, LORD. Amen.

SAY IT

I will not compare myself or our upcoming wedding with others'. Rather, I will be content in all things.

MEDITATE ON IT

"For where you have envy and selfish ambition, there you find disorder and every evil practice." (James 3:16, NIV)

"Each one should test their own actions. Then they can take pride in themselves alone, without comparing themselves to someone else, for each one should carry their own load." (Galatians 6:4–5, NIV)

"Get rid of all bitterness, rage and anger, brawling and slander, along with every form of malice." (Ephesians 4:31, NIV)

"I am not complaining about having too little. I have learned to be satisfied with whatever I have. I know what it is to be poor or to have plenty, and I have lived under all kinds of conditions. I know what it means to be full or to be hungry, to have too much or too little." (Philippians 4:11–12, CEV)

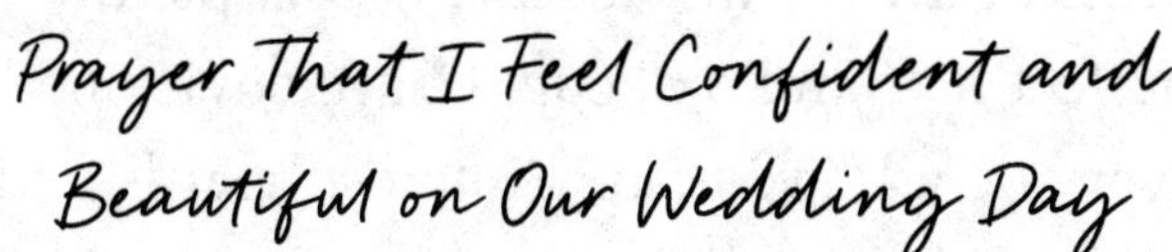

Prayer That I Feel Confident and Beautiful on Our Wedding Day

"If that is how God clothes the grass of the
field, which is here today, and tomorrow
is thrown into the fire, how much more
will He clothe you—you of little faith!
And do not set your heart on what you
will eat or drink; do not worry about it.
For the pagan world runs after all such
things, and your Father knows that you
need them. But seek His kingdom, and
these things will be given to you as well."

(Luke 12:28–31, NIV)

 *F*ather God, I have thought about our wedding day for so long. From finding the dress of my dreams to having that picture-perfect hair and makeup, I have envisioned every detail. I've made Pinterest boards and journaled about this day for years. I can't wait to walk down the aisle, LORD, but as the big day draws closer, I am a little nervous about all eyes being on me. I ask that You calm my nerves and help me to focus on the truly important aspects of the day. Help me not to get caught up in the superficial; instead, help me to meditate on the beauty and meaning of this special ceremony. And, God, help me to feel confident and beautiful, as every bride should on her wedding day. Help me not to be too critical of myself; rather, help me to see myself through Your eyes. I love You, LORD. Amen.

SAY IT

*I am a beautiful bride in every way and I am focusing
on the truly meaningful and important aspects
of our wedding day.*

MEDITATE ON IT

"Your beauty should not come from outward adornment,
such as elaborate hairstyles and the wearing of gold
jewelry or fine clothes. Rather, it should be that of your
inner self, the unfading beauty of a gentle and quiet
spirit, which is of great worth in God's sight."
(1 Peter 3:3–6, NIV)

"I praise You because I am fearfully and wonderfully made;
Your works are wonderful, I know that full well."
(Psalm 139:14, NIV)

"I delight greatly in the LORD; my soul rejoices in my God. For
He has clothed me with garments of salvation and arrayed
me in a robe of His righteousness, as a bridegroom adorns
his head like a priest, and as a bride adorns herself with
her jewels." (Isaiah 61:10, NIV)

Prayer That We Are Not Overwhelmed by All the Advice We Receive

"From the ends of the earth, I cry to
You for help when my heart is
overwhelmed. Lead me to the
towering rock of safety…"

(PSALM 61:2, NLT)

PRAY IT

*H*eavenly Father, so many well-intending people are offering their advice concerning our wedding ceremony and our marriage, and it feels overwhelming at times. LORD, help me to respond in love, even when their suggestions are not helpful, and help me not to take offense. LORD, please help me to walk in love, kindness, humility, and patience as we navigate all the advice from family, friends, and colleagues. Help us to take the good, smile through the bad, and ultimately stay true to our convictions concerning our special day and our marriage. And more than anything, LORD, help the two of us to grow closer as we navigate it all. I love You, LORD. Amen.

SAY IT

*I refuse to take offense at those offering unwanted advice,
and instead, I walk in love, kindness,
humility, and patience.*

MEDITATE ON IT

"Therefore, my dear brothers and sisters, stand firm. Let nothing move you. Always give yourselves fully to the work of the LORD, because you know that your labor in the LORD is not in vain." (1 Corinthians 15:58, NIV)

"For the LORD gives wisdom; from His mouth comes knowledge and understanding. He holds success in store for the upright, He is a shield to those whose walk is blameless, for He guards the course of the just and protects the way of His faithful ones. Then you will understand what is right and just and fair—every good path. For wisdom will enter your heart, and knowledge will be pleasant to your soul." (Proverbs 2:6–10, NIV)

"The mind governed by the flesh is death, but the mind governed by the Spirit is life and peace."
(Romans 8:6, NIV)

"When I said, 'My foot is slipping,' Your unfailing love, LORD, supported me. When anxiety was great within me, Your consolation brought me joy." (Psalm 94:18–19, NIV)

Prayer for Wisdom in Our Finances

"And my God will meet all your needs according to the riches of His glory in Christ Jesus."

(PHILIPPIANS 4:19, NIV)

PRAY IT

Heavenly Father, Your Word says to ask for wisdom, so I'm coming to You today to do just that. LORD, I need Your wisdom concerning our finances. Help me not to overspend on our wedding. Help me to place priority on being a good steward, not on trying to impress others on our wedding day. Help me to keep it all in perspective and not get swept up in the emotion of it all. And, LORD, as we join our lives together, help us to keep You at the center of all our financial decisions. Thank You for blessing us. Thank You for guiding us in this financial realm. And thank You for being a generous and loving Father. I love You, amen.

SAY IT

*I will not overspend on this wedding; rather, I will make
wise financial decisions, allowing God to direct my steps.*

MEDITATE ON IT

"Direct me in the path of Your commands, for there I find
delight. Turn my heart toward Your statutes and not
toward selfish gain. Turn my eyes away from worthless
things; preserve my life according to Your Word."
(Psalm 119:35–37, NIV)

"One person gives freely, yet gains even more; another
withholds unduly, but comes to poverty. A generous
person will prosper; whoever refreshes others will be
refreshed." (Proverbs 11:24–25, NIV)

"But since you excel in everything—in faith, in speech, in
knowledge, in complete earnestness and in the love we
have kindled in you—see that you also excel in this grace
of giving. I am not commanding you, but I want to test the
sincerity of your love by comparing it with the earnestness
of others." (2 Corinthians 8:7–8, NIV)

"Do nothing out of selfish ambition or vain conceit. Rather, in humility value others above yourselves, not looking to your own interests but each of you to the interests of the others." (Philippians 2:3–4, NIV)

"Do not store up for yourselves treasures on earth, where moths and vermin destroy, and where thieves break in and steal. But store up for yourselves treasures in heaven, where moths and vermin do not destroy, and where thieves do not break in and steal. For where your treasure is, there your heart will be also." (Matthew 6:19–21, NIV)

Prayer That God Is the Center of Our Wedding and Our Life

"And He is before all things, and in Him all things hold together."

(Colossians 1:17, ESV)

PRAY IT

*F*ather God, I want more than anything for You to be at the center of every plan we make for our wedding and every decision we make in our marriage. Help us to never lose sight of You or put aside Your Word. Instead, LORD, help us to give You first place in our relationship, today, tomorrow, and always. Let Your love fill our hearts, our wedding day, and our marriage. And keep us grounded in Your Word, guided by Your direction, and encouraged by Your promises. I pray that our wedding glorifies You and that our marriage becomes an example of Your love. Thank You, God, for this amazing season in my life. I am so grateful! I love You, God, amen.

SAY IT

*I am determined to keep God at the center of
every decision regarding our wedding and our
marriage—no matter what!*

MEDITATE ON IT

"But if serving the LORD seems undesirable to you, then choose for yourselves this day whom you will serve, whether the gods your ancestors served beyond the Euphrates, or the gods of the Amorites, in whose land you are living. But as for me and my household, we will serve the LORD." (Joshua 24:15, NIV)

"Since, then, you have been raised with Christ, set your hearts on things above, where Christ is, seated at the right hand of God. Set your minds on things above, not on earthly things. For you died, and your life is now hidden with Christ in God." (Colossians 3:1–3, NIV)

"Do not be conformed to this world, but be transformed by the renewal of your mind, that by testing you may discern what is the will of God, what is good and acceptable and perfect." (Romans 12:2, ESV)

"Commit to the LORD whatever you do, and He will establish your plans." (Proverbs 16:3, NIV)

Prayer That I Remember All the Special Aspects of the Day and Am Present in the Moment

"Therefore do not worry about tomorrow, for tomorrow will worry about itself. Each day has enough trouble of its own."

(Matthew 6:34, NIV)

$\mathcal{F}$ather God, as our wedding approaches, I realize so many details will need my attention on that day. I don't want to spend our wedding day being worried and distracted. Help me, LORD, to be present in the moment, enjoying every single aspect of the day from beginning to end. Your Word says to cast my cares onto You, so I am doing that right now, LORD. Help me not to take those worries back. Also, Father, I have heard others say they were so overwhelmed on their big day that they couldn't remember all the special moments. I want to remember, LORD, so please give me the capacity to remember every special second of that day and bask in the beauty of it all. Thank You, God, for loving me and caring about everything I care about. You are amazing. Amen.

SAY IT

*I will be present on our wedding day, basking in the
beauty of it all and cherishing those special moments.*

MEDITATE ON IT

"Cast all your anxiety on Him because He cares for you."
   (1 Peter 5:7, NIV)

"Let the peace of Christ rule in your hearts, since as members
   of one body you were called to peace. And be thankful.
   Let the message of Christ dwell among you richly as you
   teach and admonish one another with all wisdom through
   psalms, hymns, and songs from the Spirit, singing to
   God with gratitude in your hearts. And whatever you do,
   whether in word or deed, do it all in the name of the LORD
   Jesus, giving thanks to God the Father through Him."
   (Colossians 3:15–17, NIV)

"'Martha, Martha,' the LORD answered, 'you are worried and
   upset about many things, but few things are needed—or
   indeed only one. Mary has chosen what is better, and it
   will not be taken away from her.'" (Luke 10:41–42, NIV)

"You make known to me the path of life; You will fill me with
   joy in Your presence, with eternal pleasures at Your right
   hand." (Psalm 16:11, NIV)

Prayer for a Peaceful Atmosphere on Our Wedding Day

"I have told you these things, so that in Me you may have peace. In this world you will have trouble. But take heart! I have overcome the world."

(John 16:33, NIV)

PRAY IT

$\mathcal{F}$ather God, You are the author of peace,
so I am asking for Your supernatural
peace to be present on our wedding day.
Let there be a sweet atmosphere of love from
the minute the day begins until the minute
it ends. Let Your peace fill every corner of
the venue, and, LORD, let Your peace reign big
in my heart as well. I pray that everyone in
our wedding party, in our family, and among
our guests and all the vendors get along
and enjoy the day. I pray for absolutely
no strife or struggle on our big day. And I
am thanking You in advance for a tangible,
heavy presence of Your love, peace, and joy.
I love You, LORD. Amen.

SAY IT

I will walk in peace and refuse to enter into any strife or drama on our wedding day.

MEDITATE ON IT

"Let the peace of Christ rule in your hearts, since as members of one body you were called to peace. And be thankful." (Colossians 3:15, NIV)

"Blessed are the peacemakers, for they will be called children of God." (Matthew 5:9, NIV)

"I am leaving you with a gift—peace of mind and heart. And the peace I give is a gift the world cannot give. So don't be troubled or afraid." (John 14:27, NLT)

"Dear brothers and sisters, I close my letter with these last words: Be joyful. Grow to maturity. Encourage each other. Live in harmony and peace. Then the God of love and peace will be with you." (2 Corinthians 13:11, NLT)

Prayer That We Always Show Each Other Respect and Communicate in Love

"Do not let any unwholesome talk come out of your mouths, but only what is helpful for building others up according to their needs, that it may benefit those who listen."

(EPHESIANS 4:29, NIV)

PRAY IT

$\mathcal{F}$ather God, You tell us that our words hold the power to create and to destroy. As I prepare not only for our wedding but also for this new life together, teach me to choose my words with care. Help me to honor You and honor my husband in the way I speak. Guard my voice against bitter tones. Fill me with words of grace and gratitude when I feel like slipping into anger or condemnation. Let our vows become the foundation for a lifetime of love, truth, and respect for one another, knowing that these words will build a fruitful marriage. In times of trial, help me to listen. In times of pain, remind me to be truthful, and in all things, LORD, let my lips praise Your precious name for the blessing of this gift of marriage. Amen.

SAY IT

*I choose to speak words of life, even in
moments of struggle.*

MEDITATE ON IT

"From the fruit of their mouth a person's stomach is filled;
with the harvest of their lips they are satisfied. The tongue
has the power of life and death, and those who love it will
eat its fruit. He who finds a wife finds what is good and
receives favor from the LORD." (Proverbs 18:20–22, NIV)

"Instead, speaking the truth in love, we will grow to become
in every respect the mature body of Him who is the head,
that is, Christ." (Ephesians 4:15, NIV)

"However, each one of you also must love his wife as he
loves himself, and the wife must respect her husband."
(Ephesians 5:33, NIV)

"A gentle answer deflects anger, but harsh words make
tempers flare." (Proverbs 15:1, NLT)

Prayer That We Stay United Even When Life Is Busy or Hard

"To the married I give this command (not I, but the LORD): A wife must not separate from her husband."

(1 CORINTHIANS 7:10, NIV)

PRAY IT

*F*ather God, You see the chaos and craziness
in this season of life. You know how many
times our desire to create this ceremony
of unity has left us looking in opposite
directions, and You know how often our
hearts sense separation even as we look to
this next step of oneness. Today, though,
LORD, I remember Your peace. I remember
the unity You have within Yourself and pray
that Your Spirit would teach us how to come
together as one body, one heart, and one
mind. Draw us together, LORD. Teach us to
love as You love as we prepare to become one
flesh. Give us Your hope and Your direction
and allow us to be pulled toward You rather
than becoming disjointed in all the smaller
details and bigger weights of this world.
Thank You, LORD, for giving us Yourself as
an example of oneness and completeness.
Amen.

SAY IT

I will not allow any circumstances to cause division in our marriage. I choose to walk in love and seek unity through Jesus Christ.

MEDITATE ON IT

"'Haven't you read,' He replied, 'that at the beginning the Creator "made them male and female," and said, "For this reason a man will leave his father and mother and be united to his wife, and the two will become one flesh"? So they are no longer two, but one flesh. Therefore what God has joined together, let no one separate.'" (Matthew 19:4–6, NIV)

"And now these three remain: faith, hope and love. But the greatest of these is love." (1 Corinthians 13:13, NIV)

"The LORD God said, 'It is not good for the man to be alone. I will make a helper suitable for him.'" (Genesis 2:18, NIV)

"Just as a body, though one, has many parts, but all its many parts form one body, so it is with Christ." (1 Corinthians 12:12, NIV)

Prayer That Our Marriage Is Filled with Laughter, Joy, and Fun

"As a young man marries a young woman, so will your Builder marry you; as a bridegroom rejoices over his bride, so will your God rejoice over you."

(ISAIAH 62:5, NIV)

PRAY IT

Father God, thank You for this time of celebration and expectancy. Thank You for the joy that we have in one another and for this opportunity to learn more about Your love through marriage. Thank You most of all for celebrating with us! LORD, help us to choose joy in this new life, not just on our wedding day but through every day to come. Help us to remember the laughter and newness of our relationship and the way that we are not only lovers but also best friends. Keep our love from growing stale, LORD, and remind us instead of the vastness and completeness that we find first in You, and then in each other. Fill our home with love and laughter, Father, and help us to find daily the wonder and fun in marriage. I love You, God. Amen.

SAY IT

*I embrace the joy of this season and give thanks
for the gift of being a bride.*

MEDITATE ON IT

"His mouth is sweetness itself; he is altogether lovely. This
is my beloved, this is my friend, daughters of Jerusalem."
(Song of Songs 5:16, NIV)

"Let him kiss me with the kisses of his mouth—for your love
is more delightful than wine." (Song of Songs 1:2, NIV)

"This is what the LORD says: You have said, 'This is a desolate
land where people and animals have all disappeared.'
Yet in the empty streets of Jerusalem and Judah's other
towns, there will be heard once more the sounds of joy
and laughter. The joyful voices of bridegrooms and brides
will be heard again, along with the joyous songs of people
bringing thanksgiving offerings to the LORD. They will
sing, 'Give thanks to the LORD of Heaven's Armies, for
the LORD is good. His faithful love endures forever!'"
(Jeremiah 33:10–11, NLT)

"He has made everything beautiful in its time. He has also set eternity in the human heart; yet no one can fathom what God has done from beginning to end. I know that there is nothing better for people than to be happy and to do good while they live. That each of them may eat and drink, and find satisfaction in all their toil—this is the gift of God." (Ecclesiastes 3:11–13, NIV)

Prayer That Our Marriage Withstands the Storms of Life

"When you pass through the waters,
I will be with you; and through the
rivers, they shall not overwhelm you;
when you walk through fire you shall
not be burned, and the flame shall not
consume you."

(Isaiah 43:2, ESV)

PRAY IT

Father God, I know that Your Word says in this life there will be trouble. I understand that we aren't promised a life of sunshine, butterflies, and bluebirds on our shoulders, but, God, when the waves of trouble crash into our lives, help us to withstand the storms. Give us Your strength to stand up when others crumble, and use those storms to bring me and my husband even closer to You and to each other. Help us, LORD, to keep our eyes on You—no matter what. And help us to be a witness to others as we go through life's storms with grace. Father, I know that Your Word says You will use what the devil means for harm for good, so help us to stand strong as that plays out in our lives. And, lastly, help us to trust You through it all. I love You, amen.

SAY IT

*I will trust in God through every storm and keep
my eyes fixed on Him.*

MEDITATE ON IT

"Peace I leave with you; My peace I give to you. Not as
the world gives do I give to you. Let not your hearts be
troubled, neither let them be afraid." (John 14:27, ESV)

"God is our refuge and strength, always ready to help in
times of trouble." (Psalm 46:1, NLT)

"When the righteous cry for help, the LORD hears and delivers
them out of all their troubles." (Psalm 34:17, ESV)

"He calmed the storm to a whisper and stilled the waves."
(Psalm 107:29, NLT)

Prayer That I Show Love to My Future Husband, Now and Always

"Love is patient, love is kind. It does not envy, it does not boast, it is not proud. It does not dishonor others, it is not self-seeking, it is not easily angered, it keeps no record of wrongs. Love does not delight in evil but rejoices with the truth. It always protects, always trusts, always hopes, always perseveres. Love never fails."

(1 Corinthians 13:4–8, NIV)

*F*ather God, I know that Your love never fails! Your Word tells us that love is patient, kind, and keeps no record of wrongs. That it does not envy or boast, and that pride has no place in it. Love seeks the good of others, isn't easily angered, rejoices with the truth, and always protects, hopes, trusts, and perseveres. Help us to live this out every single day. God, I want our marriage to honor You, and I want our love to look like this. Grow me up, LORD, in patience and kindness and help me to see only the best in my husband. In times when it seems hard to love, help me to rest in Your unfailing love and learn from You. Bless our home with every fruit of the Spirit, that it may be a peaceful dwelling. Father, I want our marriage and our love to be built on these principles; make our love like You, for *You are love*. I love You, God, amen.

SAY IT

*I love deeply and love well. In this new chapter of love, I
will be patient, kind, honoring, selfless, and trusting.*

MEDITATE ON IT

"Let love and faithfulness never leave you; bind them around
your neck, write them on the tablet of your heart. Then
you will win favor and a good name in the sight of God
and man." (Proverbs 3:3–4, NIV)

"Hatred stirs up conflict, but love covers over all wrongs."
(Proverbs 10:12, NIV)

"But the fruit of the Spirit is love, joy, peace, forbearance,
kindness, goodness, faithfulness, gentleness and
self-control. Against such things there is no law."
(Galatians 5:22–23, NIV)

"Beloved, let us love one another, for love is from God, and
whoever loves has been born of God and knows God.
Anyone who does not love does not know God, because
God is love." (1 John 4:7–8, ESV)

Prayer That We Are Quick to Forgive Each Other and Do Not Allow Bitterness to Take Root in Our Hearts

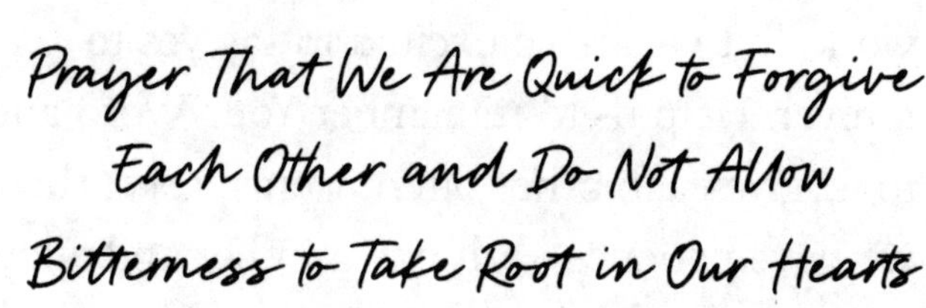

"Put on then, as God's chosen ones,
holy and beloved, compassionate
hearts, kindness, humility, meekness, and
patience, bearing with one another
and, if one has a complaint against
another, forgiving each other; as the
LORD has forgiven you, so you also
must forgive."

(COLOSSIANS 3:12–13, ESV)

Father God, as we prepare for this adventure of marriage, we know it will take work, but we are so excited to say yes to forever. Help us to remember Your Word and to forgive each other often. I pray, LORD, that we have patience with one another and allow Your love to rule in our house. And, LORD, help us to always see the best in each other. I ask You to soften our hearts in conflict and let us be quick to admit wrongdoing. You forgive us for all we do, so help us to forgive each other and not allow any bitterness to take root in our hearts. God, show us where we need to forgive, and help to draw us closer to each other and, ultimately, You. We love You and thank You for Your boundless grace and forgiveness. Amen.

SAY IT

I am patient in our marriage, learning and growing every day, and I love and forgive just as Christ has forgiven me.

MEDITATE ON IT

"My dear brothers and sisters, take note of this: Everyone should be quick to listen, slow to speak and slow to become angry." (James 1:19, NIV)

"Then Peter came to Jesus and asked, 'LORD, how many times shall I forgive my brother or sister who sins against me? Up to seven times?' Jesus answered, 'I tell you, not seven times, but seventy-seven times.'" (Matthew 18:21–22, NIV)

"The heart knows its own bitterness, and no stranger shares its joy." (Proverbs 14:10, ESV)

"Whoever covers an offense seeks love, but he who repeats a matter separates close friends." (Proverbs 17:9, ESV)

Prayer That We Develop Healthy Habits So We Can Enjoy Many Years Together

"Don't you realize that your body is the temple of the Holy Spirit, who lives in you and was given to you by God? You do not belong to yourself, for God bought you with a high price. So you must honor God with your body."

(1 Corinthians 6:19–20, NLT)

PRAY IT

𝓗eavenly Father, as Your Word says, I want to honor You with my body. Help me and my future husband to develop healthy habits so that we might live long and strong and enjoy many years of marriage. I pray that You heal our bodies and keep our minds and spirits whole. Energize us, LORD, to serve You and walk in our callings together. Renew our strength. Give us clarity of mind. And help us to make healthy decisions today so that our tomorrows are even better. I love You so much, LORD. Amen.

SAY IT

*I make healthy decisions so that I can be a better wife
to my future husband and a better daughter
of the Most High King.*

MEDITATE ON IT

" 'I will give you back your health and heal your wounds,'
says the LORD." (Jeremiah 30:17, NLT)

"Therefore, I urge you, brothers and sisters, in view of God's
mercy, to offer your bodies as a living sacrifice, holy and
pleasing to God—this is your true and proper worship."
(Romans 12:1, NIV)

"A cheerful heart is good medicine, but a crushed spirit dries
up the bones." (Proverbs 17:22, NIV)

"Do not be wise in your own eyes; fear the LORD and shun
evil. This will bring health to your body and nourishment
to your bones." (Proverbs 3:7–8, NIV)

Prayer That We Put Away Pride and Selfishness and Humbly Serve One Another

"You, my brothers and sisters, were called to be free. But do not use your freedom to indulge the flesh; rather serve one another humbly in love."

(Galatians 5:13, NIV)

PRAY IT

Father God, humility can be hard. When disagreements arise, please help us to put our pride and selfishness away, and let us be humble. Help us to serve one another and remember that we are on the same team! God, I know it is easier said than done, but I pray You will help us not to keep track of who is right or wrong but instead to be quick to say, "I'm sorry." I pray for guidance and direction for our marriage and that we work every day to keep our focus on You and Your Kingdom. Let us follow Your example, LORD, through good times and bad. I love You, God; make us Your humble servants. Thank You for all You do, amen.

SAY IT

I intentionally serve my spouse and follow
Christ's example of humility.

MEDITATE ON IT

"Do nothing out of selfish ambition or vain conceit. Rather, in humility value others above yourselves." (Philippians 2:3, NIV)

"And He sat down and called the twelve. And He said to them, 'If anyone would be first, he must be last of all and servant of all.'" (Mark 9:35, ESV)

"But He gives more grace. Therefore it says, 'God opposes the proud but gives grace to the humble.'" (James 4:6, NIV)

"When pride comes, then comes disgrace, but with humility comes wisdom." (Proverbs 11:2, ESV)

Prayer That We Have Favor Go Before Us in Every Area of Our Lives

"May the favor of the LORD our God rest on us; establish the work of our hands for us—yes, establish the work of our hands."

(PSALM 90:17, NIV)

*F*ather God, I pray that You will surround our marriage with Your great favor and bless the work of our hands as Your Word says. I pray that You will lead us and guide us and open doors for us that no man can shut. LORD, help us not to be afraid to walk through those doors that You are opening for us. I'm excited, God, for the future. I trust You with all my hopes, dreams, and plans, knowing that You have a good plan for me according to Jeremiah 29:11. Thank You for Your supernatural favor that makes a way where there seems to be no way. I'm so grateful that I can trust You in all things concerning our marriage—where we live, where we work, where we go to church, who we let into our inner circle—all things. Thank You for Your favor that lasts a lifetime, LORD. I love You. Amen.

SAY IT

The favor of God surrounds me, and I trust the
LORD in every area of my life.

MEDITATE ON IT

"Surely, LORD, You bless the righteous; You surround them
with Your favor as with a shield." (Psalm 5:12, NIV)

"For the LORD God is a sun and shield; the LORD bestows favor
and honor; no good thing does He withhold from those
whose walk is blameless." (Psalm 84:11, NIV)

"And Jesus grew in wisdom and stature, and in favor with
God and man." (Luke 2:52, NIV)

"For his anger lasts only a moment, but his favor lasts a
lifetime; weeping may stay for the night, but rejoicing
comes in the morning." (Psalm 30:5, NIV)

"'For I know the plans I have for you,' declares the LORD,
'plans to prosper you and not to harm you, plans to give
you hope and a future.'" (Jeremiah 29:11, NIV)

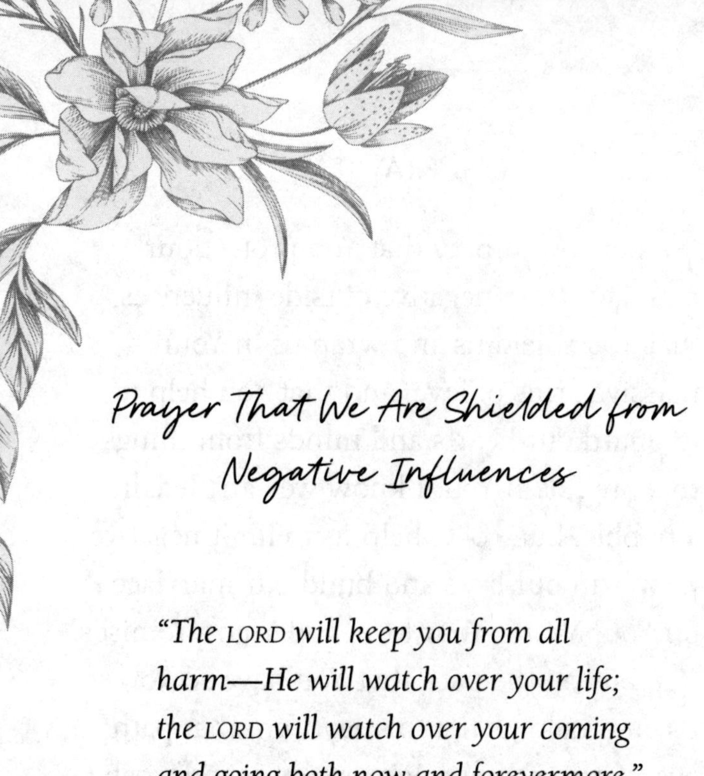

Prayer That We Are Shielded from Negative Influences

"The LORD will keep you from all
harm—He will watch over your life;
the LORD will watch over your coming
and going both now and forevermore."

(PSALM 121:7–8, NIV)

Father God, I pray that You protect our marriage from negative outside influences, that You shield us and wrap us in Your massive arms of love, and that You help us to guard our hearts and minds from things that are not of You. I know we can't live in a bubble, but, LORD, help us to limit negative people in our lives and build our marriage on Your Word, Your love, and Your promises. Keep us on the path that You have set for us, and help us not to stray from that path even for a moment. We are not afraid, LORD, but we are cautious because we realize that it's important where we spend our time and allow our thoughts to go. Plant our feet, Father God, firmly in Your Word. Keep us under Your protective wings, and draw us closer to You as we grow closer to each other. Thank You for Your protection of us—spirit, soul, and body. Amen.

SAY IT

I am careful who and what I let into my heart and marriage, following God's lead in all things.

MEDITATE ON IT

"Don't be afraid, for I am with you. Don't be discouraged, for I am your God. I will strengthen you and help you. I will hold you up with My victorious right hand." (Isaiah 41:10, NLT)

"Even when I walk through the darkest valley, I will not be afraid, for You are close beside me. Your rod and Your staff protect and comfort me." (Psalm 23:4, NLT)

"He will cover you with His feathers. He will shelter you with His wings. His faithful promises are your armor and protection." (Psalm 91:4, NLT)

"But the LORD is faithful, and He will strengthen you and protect you from the evil one." (2 Thessalonians 3:3, NIV)

"You are My hiding place; you will protect me from trouble and surround me with songs of deliverance." (Psalm 32:7, NIV)

Prayer That We Have Patience as We Learn to Be a Married Couple

"Therefore, as God's chosen people, holy and dearly loved, clothe yourselves with compassion, kindness, humility, gentleness and patience."

(Colossians 3:12, NIV)

Father God, I pray that You will give me patience with myself and my husband as we learn to mesh our lives together and live as a married couple. Help us not to take each other for granted; rather, help us to find new reasons to love each other every single day. And when conflicts arise, help me to remember all the reasons I love my husband and focus on what's really important. Let love and patience rule in our house so that we can grow together in the safety and beauty of a healthy marriage. Help us also, LORD, to be patient as we build this life together. When things don't happen as quickly as we expect, help us to remember that great things are worth the wait. We trust You in all things. I love You. Amen.

SAY IT

*I am patient with my husband and myself as we
learn to live together as one.*

MEDITATE ON IT

"Rejoice in our confident hope. Be patient in trouble, and
keep on praying." (Romans 12:12, NLT)

"The end of a matter is better than its beginning, and
patience is better than pride." (Ecclesiastes 7:8, NIV)

"Whoever is patient has great understanding, but one who is
quick-tempered displays folly." (Proverbs 14:29, NIV)

"Let us not become weary in doing good, for at the proper
time we will reap a harvest if we do not give up."
(Galatians 6:9, NIV)

Prayer That We Always Have a Sense of Adventure, Exploring This Great Life Together

"In their hearts humans plan their course, but the LORD establishes their steps."

(PROVERBS 16:9, NIV)

PRAY IT

Heavenly Father, thank You for giving me a sense of adventure and the desire to explore and never stay safely inside my comfort zone. I pray that the adventure of marriage is a good one, moving through this life, hand in hand with my husband. Give us the courage to do more than we thought we could, LORD. Help us to not be so destination-focused that we miss out on the joy of the actual journey. Keep us grounded in You, God, while also having that spirit of adventure and whimsy. Thank You for an amazing partner in this adventure. Please keep us safe and happy and whole as we gear up for what comes next. I love You, LORD. Amen.

SAY IT

I will go through this life, hand in hand with my husband,
following the path that God has for us.

MEDITATE ON IT

"But thank God! He has made us His captives and continues
to lead us along in Christ's triumphal procession. Now He
uses us to spread the knowledge of Christ everywhere,
like a sweet perfume." (2 Corinthians 2:14, NLT)

"Ask me and I will tell you remarkable secrets you do not
know about things to come." (Jeremiah 33:3, NLT)

"Jesus called out to them, 'Come, follow me, and I will show
you how to fish for people!'" (Matthew 4:19, NLT)

"You will show me the way of life, granting me the joy
of Your presence and the pleasures of living with You
forever." (Psalm 16:11, NLT)

ABOUT THE AUTHOR

Michelle Medlock Adams is an inspirational speaker and a best-selling author of more than one hundred books, including *Dinosaur Devotions*, *The Christmas Devotional*, and *Dachshund Through the Snow*. She is also a *New York Times* best-selling ghostwriter and has won more than ninety industry awards, including an ECPA Gold Medallion for *Our God is Bigger Than That!*

Michelle is married to her high school sweetheart, Jeff, and they have two married daughters, six adorable grandchildren, and two spoiled miniature dachshunds. When not writing or teaching writing, she enjoys cheering on Indiana University in sports, watching Doris Day movies, and all things leopard print. Visit her website at: www.michellemedlockadams.com.